THE ABC's: An Interactive Children's Book

ISBN 978-0-9973531-3-6

Copyright © 2017 Brandon Parker

Request for information should be addressed to:

Curry Brothers Marketing and Publishing Group
P.O. Box 247
Haymarket, VA 20168

All rights reserved. No part of this publication may be reproduced, stored in a retrieval system, or transmitted in any form or by any means, electronic, mechanical, photocopy, recording, or any other, except for brief quotations in printed reviews, without the prior permission of the publisher.

Cover by Philip Sheffield

CURRY BROTHERS MARKETING
AND PUBLISHING GROUP

Note to the parents and teachers:

Does your child or student know the alphabet?
This book will assist you in teaching
the ABCs in an easy, interactive way.
In your hands you hold 26 ways to spend time with
your child/student and have fun learning the alphabet
together. This book allows you to read the text and ask
questions. It also allows you the opportunity to add your
own questions and teachable moments to the story.

Look for my other interactive book for children titled,
"This Seasons Holidays".

For more information, classroom readings, and book
signings email: GazelleProductions@comcast.net

This book is dedicated to my mom, Dorcas.

Thank you for all your support, help, and encouragement.

A is for apple.

How many apples do you see?

B is for bubble gum.

Can you blow a bubble this big?

C is for cake.

How many candles do you see?

What kind of cake do you like?

D is for dog.

Do you have a dog?

E is for Easter eggs.

Have you ever painted Easter eggs? They are fun to paint and fun to eat.

F is for fish.

How many fish do you see?

G is for ghost.

Did you see a ghost

this past Halloween??

H is for hot chocolate.

Hot chocolate is good on a cold night. Have you ever had marshmallows in your hot chocolate?

I is for ice cream.

What's your favorite flavor of ice cream?

J is for jumping.

Do you like to jump in piles of leaves?

K is for Karate.

Have you ever taken Karate lessons?

L is for lollipop.

Do you like lollipops?

What's your favorite flavor?

M is for mittens.

Mittens keep your hands warm when it is cold outside.

What color are your mittens?

N is for nest.

This is a bird's nest.

Have you ever seen a bird's nest?

O is for oranges.

What color are they?

Do you like oranges?

P is for pizza. My favorite pizza is pepperoni.

Do you like pepperoni pizza?

Q is for quail.

A quail is a type of bird.

Have you ever seen a quail?

R is for Recycle.

Recycling is when you save things to use them again.

Have you ever recycled cans?

S

is

for

sliding.

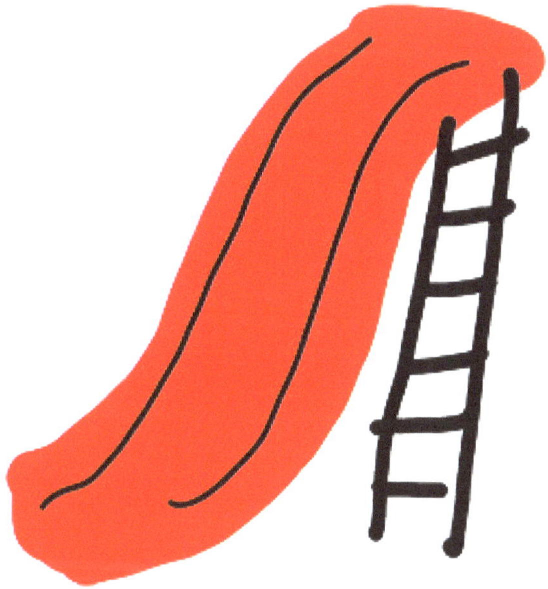

You can find slides

on playgrounds in your

neighborhood.

T is for turtle.

You can keep turtles as pets.

Have you ever had a pet turtle?

U is for umbrella.

You use umbrellas when it rains.

Do you have an umbrella?

V is for violin.

Do you like to listen to the violin?

W is for watermelon.

Have you ever eaten watermelon?

X is for x-ray.

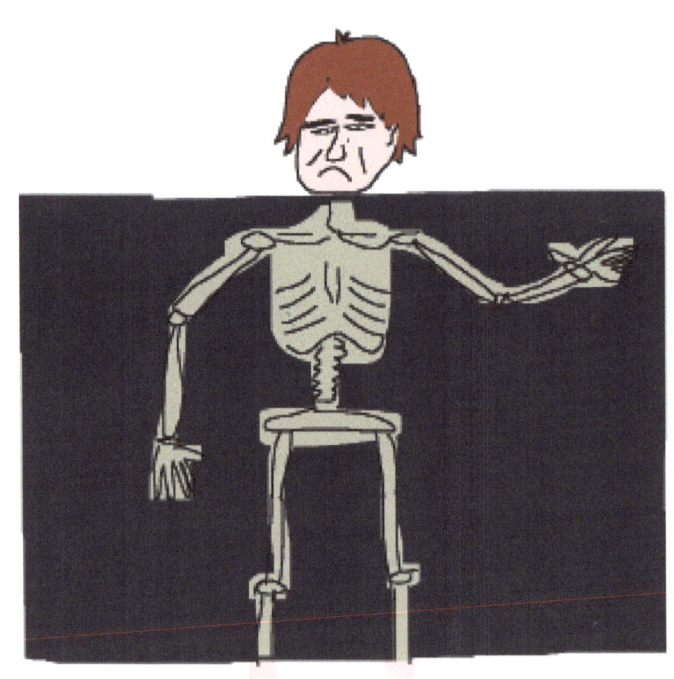

You get x-rays sometimes when you go to the doctor.

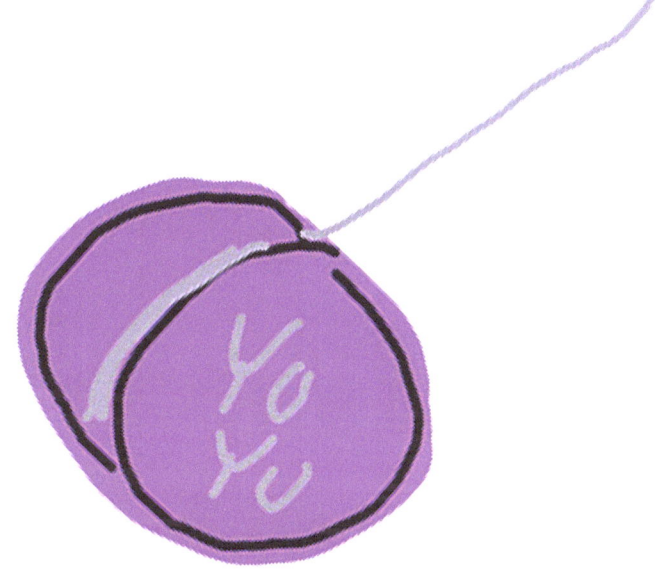

Y is for yo-yo.

Do you know how to yo-yo?

Z is for zipper,

which this shirt has none.

You've just learned

the alphabet.

Now wasn't that fun?

The End

About the Author

Brandon L. Parker is a native Nashvillian who loves singing, acting, reading, and writing. He is an actor and has performed under the acting group The NewBirth Players in the Black History play entitled "Beyond February." Parker wrote this interactive children's book and This Seasons Holidays (another interactive children's book teaching the months of the year and various holidays) during his middle school years at Two Rivers Middle School (Metropolitan Nashville Public Schools) during a youth authors project. The local newspaper, The Tennessean, featured Parker and his projects (The ABCs and Seasons). Parker is an animated reader and even read this book to a group of students at the Schrader Lane Child Care Center in Nashville while he was a student at Two Rivers Middle School. Parker also enjoys working with and encouraging youth, talking to and meeting new people.

About the Artist

Philip Sheffield Jr. (age 15) is the brother of the author, Brandon L. Parker. Sheffield has been creating various forms of artwork for more than 10 years. His drawing talents range from oil on acrylic painting and free-hand pencil drawings to computer-generated art. For this book, he used a more simplistic and childlike art style to better engage children. His other hobbies are baseball, playing the guitar, video and audio technology, skateboarding, and bike riding.

Mountains, Earth, Sky and Sea
Acrylic by Philip Sheffield Jr.
May 2015

Got an idea for a book?
Contact Curry Brothers Books, LLC. We are not satisfied until your publishing dreams come true. We specialize in all genres of books, especially religion, leadership, family history, poetry, and children's literature. There is an African Proverb that affirms, "When an elder dies, a library closes." Be careful who tells your family history. Are their values your family's values? Our staff will navigate you through the entire publishing process, and take pride in going the extra mile in meeting your publishing goals.

Improving the world, one book at a time!

CURRY BROTHERS MARKETING
AND PUBLISHING GROUP

Curry Brothers Books, LLC.
PO Box 247
Haymarket, VA 20168
(719) 466-7518 & (615) 347-9124
Visit us at www.currybrothersbooks.com

www.ingramcontent.com/pod-product-compliance
Lightning Source LLC
Chambersburg PA
CBHW041125300426
44113CB00002B/61